Mapping in the Modern World

MAPPING
THE PHYSICAL WORLD

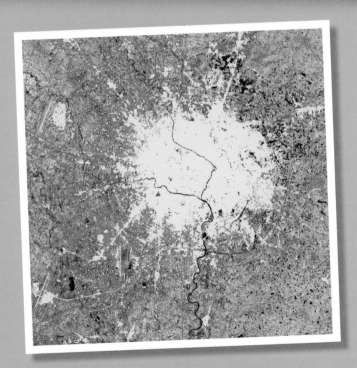

Charlie Samuels

Crabtree Publishing Company
www.crabtreebooks.com

Crabtree Publishing Company
www.crabtreebooks.com
1-800-387-7650

Published in Canada
616 Welland Ave.
St. Catharines, ON
L2M 5V6

Published in the United States
PMB 59051
350 Fifth Ave. 59th Floor
New York, NY 10118

Published in 2017 by CRABTREE PUBLISHING COMPANY

Author: Charlie Samuels

Managing Editor: Tim Cooke

Designer: Melissa Roskell

Cover Design: Katherine Berti

Picture Manager: Sophie Mortimer

Design Manager: Keith Davis

Editorial Director: Lindsey Lowe, Kathy Middleton

Editor: Janine Deschenes

Children's Publisher: Anne O'Daly

Proofreader: Ellen Rodger

**Production coordinator and
 Prepress technician:** Ken Wright

Print coordinator: Margaret Amy Salter

Produced by Brown Bear Books for
Crabtree Publishing Company

Photo credits

Photographs (t=top, b=bottom, l=left, r=right, c=center)

Front Cover: Wikimedia Commons: inset second, and third from left; All other images from Shutterstock

Interior: Australian National University's Research School of Earth Sciences (RSES): 7; Earth.com: 10; Damian Evans/Cambodian Archaeological Lidar Initiative: 27-28; Google Inc.: 13; NASA: 1, 4, 5, 6, 8, 9, 12, 19, 21, 23, 26, 27t, 30tl; NOAA: 11; Public Domain: 29; RatheeshKumar et al., Precambrian Research, In Press: 17; Robert Hurt/IPAC/Bill Saxton/NRAO/AUI/NSF: 20; Shutterstock: Tim Roberts Photography 14; USGS: 15, 30br; Wikipedia: 16, 18, 22, 24, 30tr.
All other photos, artwork and maps, Brown Bear Books.

Brown Bear Books has made every attempt to contact the copyright holder. If you have any information please contact licensing@brownbearbooks.co.uk

Library and Archives Canada Cataloguing in Publication

Samuels, Charlie, 1961-, author
    Mapping the physical world / Charlie Samuels.

(Mapping in the modern world)
Includes index.
Issued in print and electronic formats.
ISBN 978-0-7787-3236-5 (hardcover).--
ISBN 978-0-7787-3242-6 (softcover).--
ISBN 978-1-4271-1885-1 (HTML)

1. Cartography--Juvenile literature. 2. Physical geography--Juvenile literature. 3. Physical geography--Maps--Juvenile literature. 4. Historical geography--Juvenile literature. I. Title.

GA105.6.S26 2017   j526   C2016-907127-8
                                        C2016-907128-6

Library of Congress Cataloging-in-Publication Data

Names: Samuels, Charlie, 1961- author, cartographer.
Title: Mapping the physical world / Charlie Samuels.
Description: New York, NY : Crabtree Publishing Company, 2017. | Series: Mapping in the Modern World | Includes index.
Identifiers: LCCN 2017002070 (print) | LCCN 2017003673 (ebook) | ISBN 9780778732365 (reinforced library binding : alk. paper) | ISBN 9780778732426 (pbk. : alk. paper) | ISBN 9781427118851 (Electronic HTML)
Subjects: LCSH: Cartography. | Physical geography--Maps. | Landforms--Maps. | LCGFT: World atlases.
Classification: LCC G1046.B7 S2 2017 (print) | LCC G1046.B7 (ebook) | DDC 526--dc23
LC record available at https://lccn.loc.gov/2017002070

Printed in Canada/052017/TL20170327

Contents

SATELLITE SYSTEMS

The invention of satellites that orbit Earth, capturing images and collecting data, has transformed the way cartographers map the physical world.

The **Soviet Union** launched the first artificial satellite, Sputnik, into space in 1957. It orbited, or circled, Earth, 358 miles (577 km) above the planet surface. The first satellite to take images was Landsat, launched by the United States in 1972. The images gave geographers a new view of the planet—the view from space. In 1976, photographs from Landsat 1 revealed an uninhabited, or empty, island off the coast of Canada. Cartographers named it Landsat Island.

This image from Landsat 8 shows the location of tiny Landsat Island, northeast of Labrador in Canada.

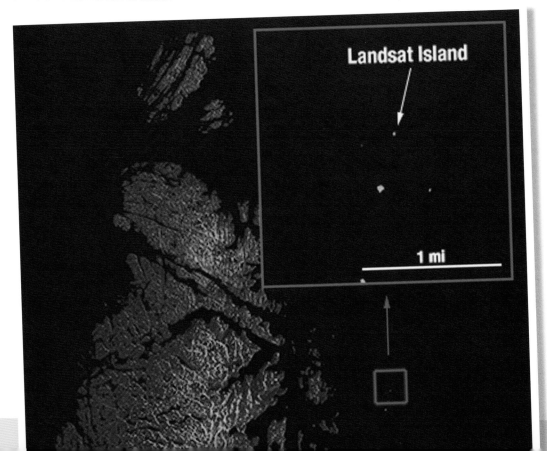

Landsat Island

1 mi

Today, around 2,200 satellites orbit Earth at different heights. They take many thousands of images, collecting data on subjects as varied as how household **aerosols** interact with the **ozone** layer to smoke pollution caused by crop burning.

The View from Space

Since its launch in 1972, NASA's Landsat program has been continually mapping Earth. It has mapped growing urbanization, melting ice caps, **deforestation**, and coastal **erosion**. The program helps cartographers map things that are difficult to see from the ground, such as shrinking coral reefs. Landsat images have also revealed unknown details, such as the head of the Lambert Glacier in Antarctica, the world's largest glacier. Landsat 8 was launched in 2013 and was scheduled to stay in service until 2021.

Landsat 8 was launched in February 2013. The large solar panels generate energy to power the satellite's scientific instruments.

My Changing Town

Maps and Me

How has your town changed over the years? Ask if your local library has old maps of the town. Compare how it looks on a map today with how it looked 10, 20, or even 100 years ago. Has it gotten bigger? Can you figure out why any new construction was located where it is?

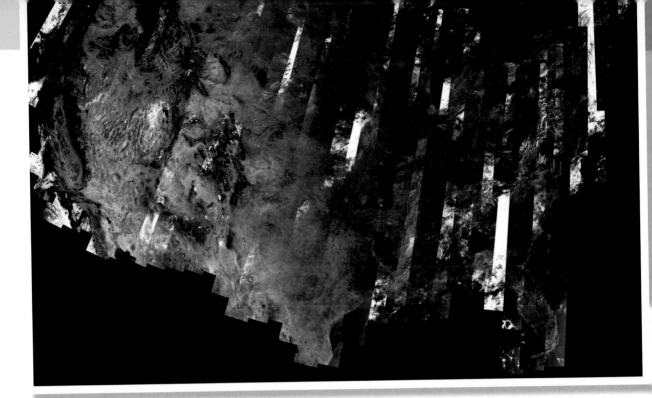

How Does Landsat Work?

Landsat satellites orbit 438 miles (705 km) above Earth. They take 99 minutes to complete one orbit. If they traveled slower, they would crash back to Earth. The satellite's orbit takes it above a different strip of Earth each time as the planet rotates. It completes 14 orbits a day. The way the satellite's orbit varies means it can photograph the whole surface of the planet every 16 days.

What has Landsat Seen?

By using images Landsat has taken of the same places over more than 40 years, cartographers have made multi-layered maps of how Earth is physically changing. They have divided the entire surface of the globe into square cells, each of which has sides 820 feet (250 m) long. The cartographers use **Geographic Information Systems** (GIS) to combine Landsat information about each cell, called "ecological land units," into layers that can be displayed on a map. The maps might contain information about soil, climate, elevation, vegetation, and land use.

On each orbit, Landsat photographs a 115-mile (185-km) strip of Earth's surface, as seen in this combined image of the United States. It takes 233 orbits, or 16 days, to cover the whole of Earth.

Did You Know?

GIS are computer programs that collect data and convert it so it can be shown in map form. Information is displayed on many different layers. Experts choose which layers they want to use to create a specific map.

In the Real World

Acting on Information

Today, flooding occurs more regularly around the world than it did in the past. Many countries use evidence from past floods to produce digital maps that show the potential future flood risks of rivers and other bodies of water. These maps also show where homes are at the greatest risk of damage from flooding.

The individual maps created for each ecological land unit can then be combined digitally into larger maps. Cartographers use Landsat maps to compare small areas to the same area on earlier maps. Such comparisons can lead to change in the real world, because cartographers can provide information about environmental changes and assess the risk for disasters. For example, Landsat photographs of the destruction of the Amazon rainforest convinced the Brazilian government to take action to stop illegal logging, or cutting down trees to sell. On a global scale, satellite evidence that the ice caps are melting and sea levels rising helped to persuade nations to take steps to reduce **global warming**, such as signing the **Paris Agreement** in 2016.

This satellite map shows flooding in the Philippines in 2011. The flooded areas (blue) are along two rivers (dark blue). The size of the blue circles indicates how many people live in each region.

HUMAN IMPACT ON EARTH

Human activity has always impacted the physical landscape of Earth. Digital maps allow experts to study how human activity leads to environmental change across the globe.

Over 2,000 years ago, an ancient Greek philosopher named Theophrastus suggested that if forests were cut down, more sunlight would reach the ground. He said that would make the land become warmer. Today, some experts, such as environmental scientists, believe that human activity such as cutting down forests can seriously harm the environment. Others argue that human activity has little effect compared to natural changes. Today, maps are one of the key tools scientists use to study **climate change** and its causes.

This Landsat image shows the growth of Chengdu, a city in China. The yellow areas show its size in 1990. The orange areas show its growth 10 years later.

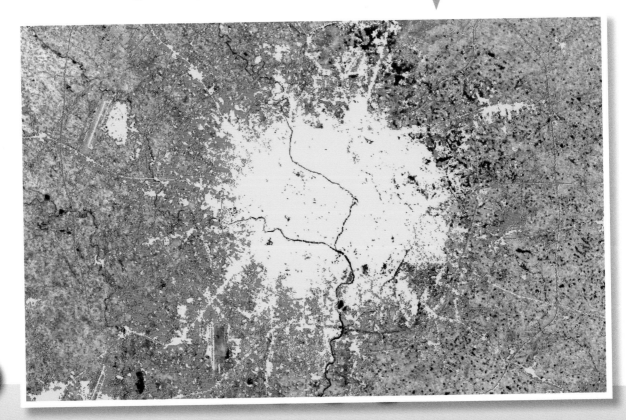

Industrial Revolution

It was not until the Industrial Revolution, which started in Great Britain in the 1700s, that human activity took place on a large enough scale to impact the global environment. The Industrial Revolution was a time when machines began to do more tasks, and manufacturing became concentrated in factories and factory towns. Machines, steam engines, and locomotives all burned coal to generate power. **Soot** particles from the coal hung in the air. One result was thick fogs that made it impossible to see in cities. In London, England, these fogs were common until burning coal for fuel was banned in 1956. The damage caused to the atmosphere by coal smoke was one of the first causes of climate change.

Did You Know?

Maps are key to the study of ecology, or the relationships between living things. Experts map different biomes, or landscapes where plants and animals are closely linked. This helps them understand the workings of the natural world.

The Ozone Layer

It was only in the late 1900s that satellites gave scientists proof of how human activity was damaging Earth. In the 1970s, scientists noticed that the ozone layer was shrinking. The ozone layer is a band of gas in the **stratosphere**, 12 to 19 miles (20–30 km) above Earth.

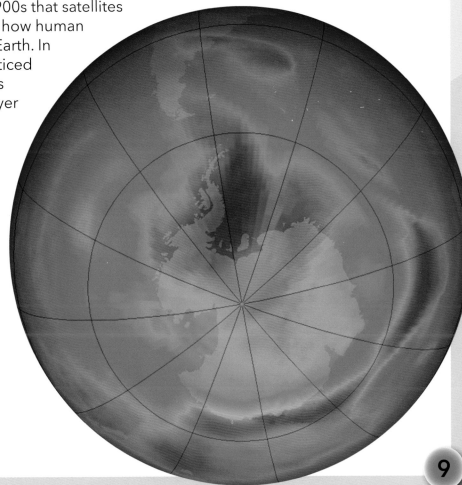

Satellites measure the depth of the ozone gas layer around Earth. The blue colors show where the ozone is at its thinnest, above the South Pole.

The ozone helps shield Earth from harmful **ultraviolet radiation** that occurs in sunlight. The maps showed that holes were appearing in the ozone layer above the North and South poles.

Having mapped the growing holes, scientists urged governments to act. To prevent further damage, governments banned the use of ozone-damaging chemicals in gases in spray cans, refrigeration systems, and air-conditioning systems. More recent satellite imagery shows that the ozone layer has begun to recover. Experts believe it will recover completely within 50 years.

Human Impact on the Land

For thousands of years, people have changed the landscape by cutting down trees, burning fires, and damming rivers.

In the Real World

Mapping the Ice Caps

Since 2008, NASA's Operation IceBridge has used airplanes to map the changing mass of the ice cap in Antarctica. The team monitors how much sea ice extends off the coast of the continent, and how much the **ice shelves** shrink over time. Melting ice shelves lead to a rise in global sea levels. This can cause flooding of communities and the loss of coastal habitats.

This map shows the ice around Antarctica in summer 2016. The whitest areas show the thickest ice. The extent of the sea ice in 2016 was the smallest ever recorded.

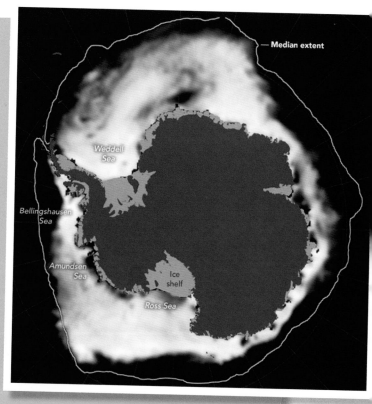

— Median extent

Weddell Sea

Bellingshausen Sea

Amundsen Sea

Ice shelf

Ross Sea

Modeling the Future

Breakthroughs

Scientists predict that rising sea levels in the next 50 years will impact low-lying countries and coastal areas. The National Oceanic and Atmospheric Administration has created an interactive map of the United States where users can zoom in on part of the coast. Move the slider to simulate the effects of varying heights of sea level rises. The map can be found at: **https://coast.noaa.gov/digitalcoast/tools/slr**

Today, a combination of rapid population growth and the spread of industrialization has greatly increased human impact on the planet. The pressure for increased areas of farmland to feed the world's growing population has led to deforestation in areas such as the Amazon, Indonesia, Borneo, and Russia. Since the late 1970s, satellite mapping has recorded these disappearing forests.

This map of Tampa Bay in Florida shows areas that would be flooded (light blue) by a 4-foot (1.2-m) rise in sea level.

The world's huge forests are vital to the environment. Forests remove carbon dioxide and other harmful gases from the air and release oxygen, which people need to breathe. Satellite maps have helped raise awareness of the need to stop illegal logging and forest clearance.

The Earth's Water

Scientists are also worried about Earth's **hydrology**, or its oceans, seas, and rivers. Satellite imaging and mapping have shown that higher global temperatures are melting the ice caps. In tropical regions, the sea has become warmer. This damages coral reefs and the plants and animals that live there. Inland, meanwhile, farming and logging along rivers destroys the roots that hold the soil in place. The soil is blown by the wind into rivers, which deposit it as silt at their mouths. Silting can change the course of rivers, and damage the communities that depend on them.

Many experts believe that rapid industrialization in China and India has contributed to a rise in global temperatures. As a result of these changes, both countries suffer increasingly frequent **monsoons**, or heavy seasonal rains.

Did You Know?

Some people do not believe that climate change is taking place. The vast majority of experts, however, believe that human activity is harming the environment. One result is a general rise in temperature, known as global warming.

This 2016 satellite map shows the extent of flooding along the Ganges River in India. The flooding was caused by unusually heavy monsoon rains.

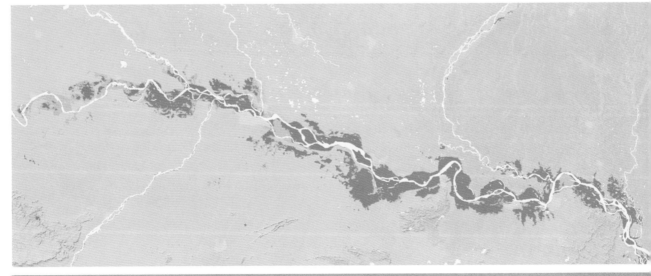

A Case Study in Change

About 2,000 years ago, Ephesus was an important city and port, or shipping center, in the Roman province of Asia Minor. The city became wealthy from trade, which was based on its harbor at the mouth of the Cayster River. However, farming along the river caused soil erosion, which filled the river with silt. The Cayster deposited this silt where it met the sea, filling up its own mouth. Ships could no longer reach Ephesus, and the harbor was moved 6 miles (9.6 km) downriver to be near the sea. Ships began to use other ports, and the city of Ephesus was soon abandoned.

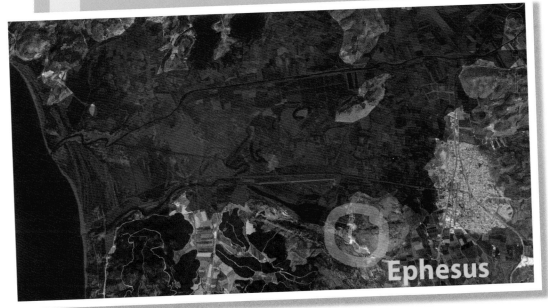

Ephesus

In 2016, India and China suffered from severe flooding. In India, the Ganges River flooded, killing more than 300 people and affecting more than six million people by destroying their homes or businesses. In China, the Yangtze River flooded in the summer of 2016, when China was struck by Cyclone Nepartak. One hundred and twenty-eight people died, and 40,000 homes and 3.7 million acres (1.09 million ha) of crops were destroyed.

This map re-creates the coastline near ancient Ephesus. The silted-up valley (purple) is now farmland, and the town is miles from the coastline (far left).

EARTH'S RESOURCES

Humans have always explored the world to find and exploit Earth's natural resources. For thousands of years, they have relied on maps to help them.

The first known map of Earth's resources is also one of the earliest maps drawn for **navigation**. The Turin **Papyrus** Map from ancient Egypt was created in around 1160 B.C.E. The map shows the route to a part of the **Egyptian** desert that had supplies of bekhen stone—a highly prized stone used to carve statues of the Egyptian kings. The map showed the location of the stone **quarries**, as well as the course of a dry riverbed called the Wadi Hammamat, a village, and ranges of hills in the area.

An open-pit copper mine in Arizona. Mining companies use maps of Earth's rocks to try to figure out likely locations to dig for minerals.

The First Nationwide Geological Map

The Egyptian quarry route map showed where specific rocks could be found. It was several centuries before people began to map general **geology**. As a boy in the late 1700s, the British **surveyor** William Smith found **fossils** near his home in the countyside. He also noticed layers of rocks called **strata**. As an adult, he discovered that the same rock strata appeared all around England. Smith realized that these were sedimentary rocks, formed by silt that had been left behind by water. He guessed that the layers always occurred in the same order, and that they could be identified from the fossils they contained. Smith used these observations to create a geological map of England, Wales, and parts of Scotland.

This map shows the age of the rocks beneath North America. The oldest rock is colored red, followed by blue, then green. The youngest rocks are colored yellow.

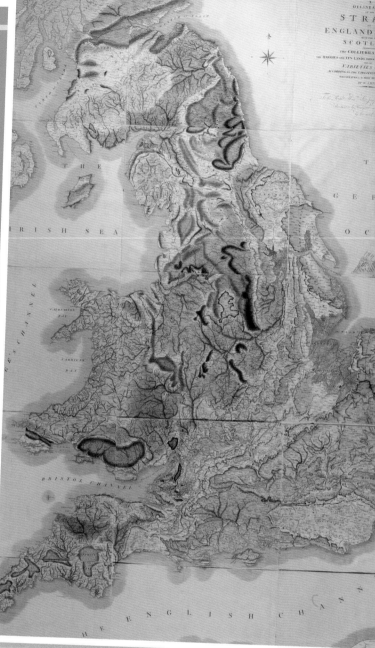

Mapping Underground

Breakthroughs

William Smith's map of England and Wales was published in 1815. The map was drawn using only his own observations at ground level. Smith noted rock strata patterns on his travels around England, and figured out that the occurrences of each rock were probably linked. He also realized that younger rocks rested on top of older rocks. By coloring each rock separately, Smith created a map that changed history.

The map came at a key time in British history. Smith's map identified where miners were likely to find coal and other **minerals** that were essential to the Industrial Revolution.

Going Underground

Since the Industrial Revolution, mining has changed greatly. Guidelines help limit the environmental impact of mines by preventing land being dug up unnecessarily. Satellite mapping helps experts decide when land should or should not be dug up. Earlier satellites could not detect geological information about rocks and metals deep underground.

William Smith's map was the first record of the different rock strata beneath the ground in Great Britain.

But newer projects such as the Global Mineral Resource Assessment Project, which began in 2002, use **radar** and **infrared** technology on satellites. They look beneath the surface of Earth and beneath the oceans. They can locate metal **ore** deposits such as gold, copper, and iron.

As Earth's resources become more scarce, or less available, mining companies are trying to find new sources of metals. They use satellite maps that use technology such as ASTER (Advanced Spaceborne Thermal Emissions and Reflection Radiometer), which was launched in December 1999. These maps allow companies to look for new sources of metals in regions such as Iran and western Pakistan.

This map shows the Biligirirangana Hills in southern India. The symbols show where geologists have done tests to map the different rocks in the area to help them find mineral deposits.

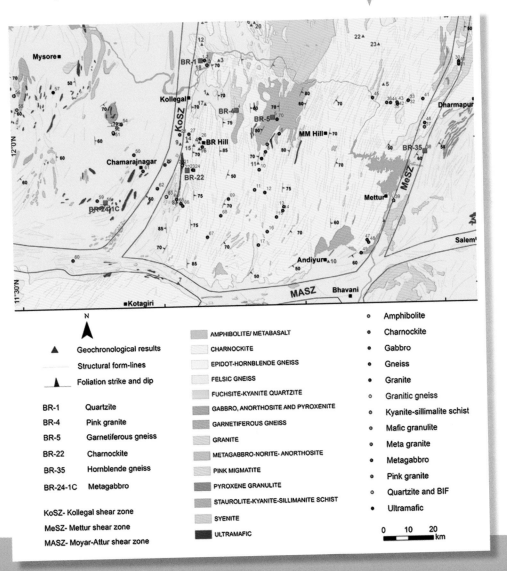

Maps and Me

Treasure Maps

One of the most valuable resources is gold—and almost everyone has heard stories of pirate treasure maps. These maps are said to have an "X" marking the spot where the treasure is buried. In fact, no genuine pirate maps have ever been found to exist. The idea seems to have come from *Treasure Island*, an adventure novel about pirates written by the Scottish author Robert Louis Stevenson in 1883.

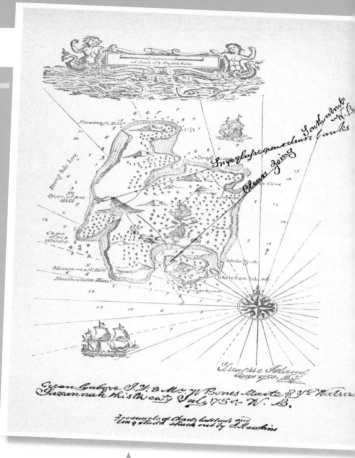

Mapping the Oceans

Mapping the ocean floor is an advancement made possible by the improvements in satellite technology. Until the late 1900s, the bed of the ocean was unexplored because it lies up to 6.8 miles (10.9 km) beneath the ocean's surface. Modern satellite technology is sophisticated enough to be able to photograph the ocean floor from space. In 2014, cartographers used satellite data to produce the most detailed map of the ocean floor. It showed ridges, trenches, and underwater volcanoes for the first time.

As well as helping experts to understand Earth's geology, mapping the oceans also has business potential. Oil companies are hoping to find new sources of oil underwater. They use satellite maps to search the **continental shelves** of Australia and the Caspian Sea for oil-drilling possibilities.

Robert Louis Stevenson drew this treasure map with his stepson. It gave him the idea for his book *Treasure Island*.

Did You Know?

Ridges in the ocean floor mark the edges of Earth's tectonic plates. These plates are sections of the planet's crust, or outer shell, that float on top of Earth's mantle, a layer of semi-molten rock. Ridges form as new rock rises up through cracks between the tectonic plates.

No Limits

Satellite mapping helps all kinds of industrial, scientific, and academic research. The data provided by satellite instruments that measure the makeup of the physical world can be used to produce a whole range of maps. Those maps will help experts find Earth's precious resources and, at the same time, can enable them to preserve as much of Earth's fragile environment as possible. This benefits not just the current generation, but will also benefit future generations, too.

Breakthroughs

Topographical Engineers

Topography is the study of the landscape. In 1838, the U.S. Army formed the Corps of Topographical Engineers to study the best places to build forts and other military facilities. The Corps explored and mapped many regions of the West. It also helped to find the best routes for wagon trails. Later, the Corps was responsible for mapping routes for railroads and highways that shaped the growth of the West.

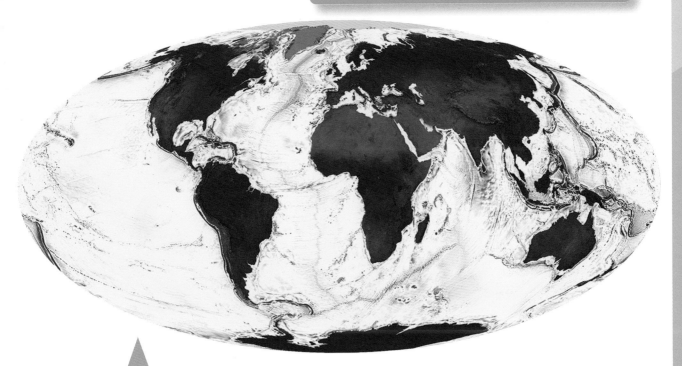

This 2014 map of the ocean floor was created by measuring gravity, which is greater in shallower regions (red and yellow) and less in deeper parts of the sea (blue).

MAPPING SPACE

Mapping space has revolutionized our understanding of the universe. Distant parts of the universe are billions of years old, so mapping them is like mapping time.

Since 2000, the Sloan Digital Sky Survey (SDSS) has created detailed 3D maps of the universe. It uses telescopes, cameras, and **spectrometers** to create its maps. Space scientists involved in the project wanted to see if the Universe was continuing to expand, and to search for planets beyond our solar system. They also hoped to locate **dark energy**. The maps show that the Milky Way (the galaxy that contains our solar system) is on the edge of a group of galaxies named Laniakea. The experts figured out that Laniakea is 500 million light-years across (a light year is the distance light can travel in a year). By mapping its farthest stars, the SDSS is mapping light that is millions of years old!

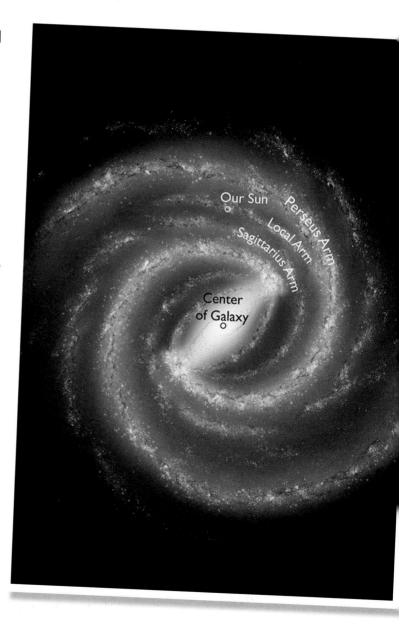

Our Sun
Perseus Arm
Local Arm
Sagittarius Arm
Center of Galaxy

This image of the Milky Way shows the location of Earth's sun in one arm of the spiral galaxy.

Mapping Background Radiation

In 1964, scientists discovered that space is full of **microwaves** coming from every direction. They call this Cosmic Microwave Background Radiation (CMBR). They have figured out that CMBR is all that remains of the energy created by the Big Bang, a massive explosion that is thought to have brought the universe into existence about 13.7 billion years ago. By mapping CMBR, scientists hope to better understand the Big Bang.

The Milky Way

In 2014, scientists completed the first digital map of the Milky Way from Earth's Northern Hemisphere. To make the map, they used 10 radio telescopes in a system that stretched from Hawaii to the Virgin Islands. Called the Very Long Baseline Array (VLBA), the telescopes used radio waves, which can see through space dust in a way other telescopes cannot. The map gave scientists more detailed measurements about the size and shape of the Milky Way galaxy.

This 2003 map taken by radio telescope shows microwave light in the Universe that originated only 380,000 years after the Big Bang that created the Universe. The map also showed that the Universe is still expanding.

Breakthroughs

Naming the Features of the Moon

In 1610, the Italian scientist Galileo Galilei looked at the moon through a telescope and drew it. He named the features he saw. Over the next centuries, other people named other parts of the Moon, usually after features on Earth. This has not always worked. The Seas of Rain and Tranquility, for example, are now known not be seas at all, but are large flat plains filled with lava.

This map of the moon was drawn in 1707. The shaded areas are low-lying plains. The white circles are round craters on the surface.

Mission to Mars

As well as mapping deep space, scientists have also successfully mapped planets in our solar system, including Mars. To date, they have created high-resolution images of almost 90 percent of Mars and made them available online.

Mapping Mars is not new. The first map of the "Red Planet" appeared in 1831. By studying the different maps produced of Mars over time, it is possible to trace how thinking about the planet has changed. The most up-to-date maps of Mars are created using

This landscape on Mars was photographed by the rover Curiosity, which began to travel over the planet's surface in 2012.

information from satellites above the planet and **rovers** on the surface. These robots have revealed that water once flowed there. Experts have learned that Mars is older than they thought, but earthquakes took place and volcanoes erupted until more recently than they thought.

Future Goals

The next goal for the exploration of Mars is to map the gases in its atmosphere. That might help to reveal what causes its swirling dust storms. The distribution of chemicals on Mars might also reveal whether any life-forms ever existed there. This kind of detailed mapping of planets beyond our solar system might one day reveal the existence of other life-forms in the Universe.

Breakthroughs

Conditions for Life

Scientists have mapped Earth's closest neighbors, including Mercury, Venus, Mars, and the Moon. By analyzing the maps, they hope to learn more about Earth's development. Each planet has its own geological history and make-up. Learning more about them might help scientists to understand how Earth would react to, say, a collision with an asteroid, a lump of rock floating in space.

MAPPING THE PAST

Because the physical landscape changes over time, mapping Earth often involves mapping the past. New developments using infrared satellites help to uncover past secrets.

In 1832, a British amateur geologist named John Auldjo produced a multi-colored map to show the lava flows from 27 eruptions of Mount Vesuvius in Italy. The colored layers show how lava in the past flowed in similar directions. It helps to explain why an eruption of Vesuvius in 79 C.E. buried the Roman cities of Pompeii and Herculaneum, which were near the base of the volcano.

John Auldjo mapped laval flows from Vesuvius, the volcano that destroyed Pompeii in 79 C.E.

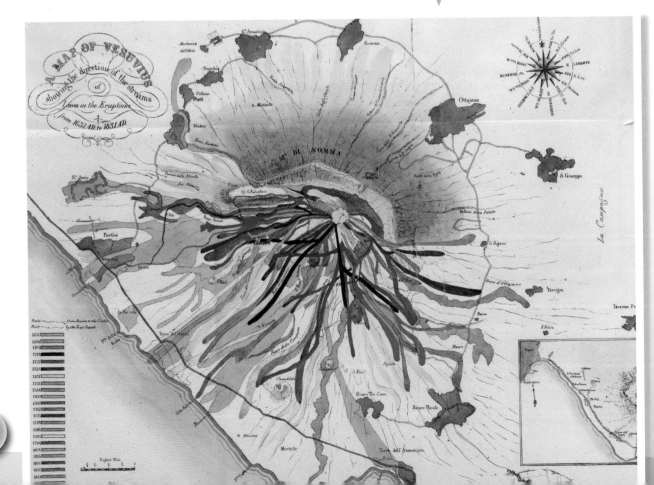

Ancient channel

Mississippi River

Oxbow lake

In the 1940s, Harold Fisk spent three years compiling a map of the Lower Mississippi River. He looked at aerial views and studied soil samples. For the first time, the map revealed the history of the river's changing channels.

Digging into the Past

Today, cartographers can look below Earth's surface. Satellites carry instruments such as infrared and X-ray cameras that can penetrate dense foliage, soil, and rock to show what is buried beneath. These satellites have revolutionized archaeology, which is the study of the past.

This satellite photograph of the course of the Mississippi River reveals clues about where the river flowed in the past.

Maps and Me

Can You See the Past?

If you can, find a map of your neighborhood. Are there any features that look strange? If a road takes a sudden detour, it may be because a building used to stand in its way. Empty strips might show an old river course or railroad tracks. Street names such as "Farm Road" might also reflect how an area looked in the past.

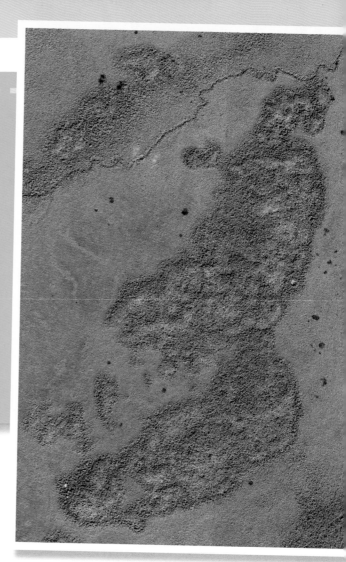

Traces of the Past

Experts use the landscape to figure out clues about how people lived in the past. They note small details, such as field boundaries, rows of trees or shrubs, or unusual ridges or mounds in the earth. They also look for unusual arrangements of rock that might not be natural. All of these features may be signs of human activity. Using satellites armed with radar and other cameras makes it far easier to spot the clues.

This infrared image in Guatemala shows forest (red) hiding evidence of Maya settlement (yellow–green) that would not be visible from the ground.

Archaeologists used to spend decades searching for lost sites where artifacts from the past can be found. Now, with today's satellites and improved high-resolution cameras, archaeologists can precisely map an area without having to uncover it.

How Does it Work?

Images made by satellite technology can show signs of ancient cities, such as chemical changes in the soil caused by building and human activity. To date, archaeologists have used satellite imaging to discover around 3,000 settlements, 1,000 lost tombs, and traces of 17 pyramids that once stood in ancient Egypt. In the early 2000s, the resolution of satellite images greatly improved. In the past, blowing up images resulted in many features becoming a blur of **pixels**. Now, these images are sharper. This allows archaeologists to zoom in on a smaller area than had previously been possible.

Archaeologists call satellite technology remote sensing. It has changed their ideas about the Maya of Central America, for example. The Maya lived in cities in northern Guatemala and southern Mexico between 2000 B.C.E. and the 800s C.E. Much of their former territory is now covered by dense jungle that would take years to explore. Using satellite technology, experts have found lost paths and roads built by the Maya. These paths likely led to cities that are now lost— but archaeologists soon hope to find them. Such discoveries can show how humans of the past left their impact on the physical world we know today.

Did You Know?

Satellite photography has sped up archaeology. In the past, it was a slow process locating lost civilizations. When Howard Carter opened the tomb of the pharaoh Tutankhamun in Egypt in 1922, he had been searching for it for 17 years!

This image shows the regular layout of ancient Khmer buildings now covered by thick forest in Cambodia.

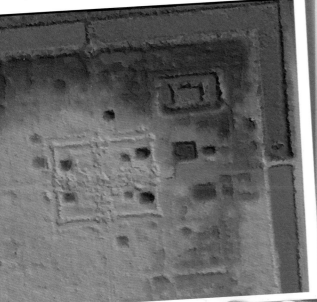

Breakthroughs

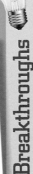

A Hidden City

When French archaeologists visited Angkor in the jungles of Cambodia in the late 1800s, it was the result of a century of study. Angkor was the capital of the Khmer people in the 1100s. Today, archaeologists study Angkor using Lidar, a remote-sensing technology that fires laser beams every four seconds and uses their reflections to map the ground. In only a few weeks, Lidar revealed signs of even older hidden cities near Angkor.

MAPS IN YOUR WORLD

There are many different ways to map the physical world around you. The map you create depends on the information you are trying to show.

Parks, creeks, and woods are aspects of the physical world we come across every day. So is a hill you can race down on your bike—but that you have to walk back up. How would you map your physical surroundings? You could try drawing your neighborhood in a way that shows the relief, or different heights, of its land. You could use old maps to try coloring areas that were once woodland or fields. You could ask older members of your family about areas that have flooded in the past and color them on a map to show what areas might flood again in the future.

However you make your map, it will be unique. No two people have identical goals and interests, so no two people will draw the same map.

This map (below) shows railroads (red) and cable cars (black) on the Jungfrau mountain in the Alps in Switzerland. It paints the mountain and its foothills in relief to give an idea of their respective heights.

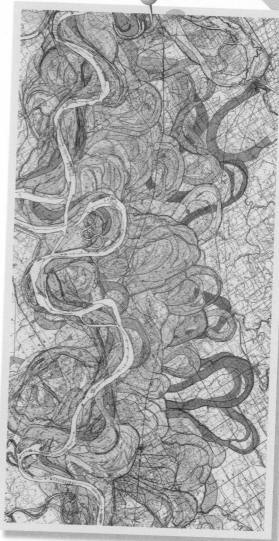

These are a satellite map of the Mississippi River (above) and a drawn map of the river's former channels (above right). Try taking photographs of parts of a body of water you are familiar with, such as a small lake, pond, river, or creek, then assemble them to make a map—or try drawing it in detail just from observation.

This map (right) combines a map of Manhattan in 1867 (far right) with one from 1967 (left). Try comparing old and new maps of your own neighborhood to see how it has changed.

Glossary

aerosols A liquid substance in a sealed pressurized can that can be sprayed out with a gas

cartographers People who make and study maps

climate change The impact of humans on Earth's climate, causing it to become gradually warmer

continental shelves Areas of seabed around continents where the sea is relatively shallow

dark energy An unseen type of energy that experts think makes up most of the universe

deforestation The widespread clearing of trees and depletion of forests

Egyptian (desert) The Eastern and Western deserts that flank the country of Egypt

erosion The process by which land is worn away by wind, rain, or water

environmentalists People who want to protect the natural world

fossils The remains of prehistoric plants and animals preserved in rock

Geographic Information Systems Computer programs that use a wide range of sources to generate maps

geology The study of the rocks that make up Earth

global warming An increase in Earth's overall temperature

hydrology The study of Earth's water and its relationship with land

ice shelves Floating sheets of ice that are attached to a piece of land

infrared Describes a type of radiation with a high wavelength that is not visible to the human eye

microwaves Electromagnetic energy with a short wavelength

minerals Hard, naturally occurring substances that are extracted from the ground for people to use

monsoons Rains carried by winds that blow regularly at certain times of the year in South and Southeast Asia

navigation Finding one's position and figuring out a route

ore Rock from which metals or minerals can be obtained

ozone A gas that forms a layer high in the atmosphere that protects Earth from harmful radiation

papyrus A writing material, similar to paper, made from fibers from reeds

Paris Agreement An agreement between nations to combat climate change by reducing greenhouse gas emissions, starting in 2020.

pixels Tiny dots of light that create a picture on a computer or TV screen

port A town or city with a harbor used for transportation by water

quarries Places where rocks are dug out of the ground

radar A device for locating objects by bouncing radio waves off them

rovers Vehicles designed to explore the surface of planets, moons, and other space bodies

satellites Artificial bodies that orbit Earth in order to collect information

silt Fine sand or clay deposited by a river

soot A powdery black substance created by burning something

Soviet Union A former communist country in eastern Europe and northern Asia governed by Russia

spectrometers Devices that measure light and other forms of energy

strata The layers of rock that make up Earth

stratosphere The upper layer of Earth's atmosphere

surveyor Someone who carefully studies and maps land

ultraviolet radiation Waves of electromagnetic energy that are not visible to the eye

On the Web

coast.noaa.gov/digitalcoast/ tools/slr
A site where users can find out for themselves the effects of future sea rise on coastal communities.

https://www.nasa.gov/mission_ pages/mars/images/index.html
A page featuring the latest images from NASA's mission to explore the surface of Mars.

http://www.onegeology.org/ eXtra/kids/maps.html
An introduction for children to maps that illustrate Earth's geology.

http://www.climatehotmap.org
A site that uses satellite photographs and maps to show the effects of climate change.

http://climatekids.nasa.gov/
A NASA site that explains the effects of climate change on Earth and on all areas of our daily lives.

Books

Berry, Jill K, and Linden McNeilly. *Map Art Lab: 52 Exciting Explorations in Mapmaking, Imagination, and Travel.* Lab Series. Quarry Books, 2014.

National Geographic Kids World Atlas. National Geographic Children's, 2013.

Panchyk, Richard. *Charting the World: Geography and Maps from Cave Paintings to GPS with 21 Activities.* Chicago Review, 2011.

Peetoom, Laura, and Paul Heersink. *Maps and Mapping for Canadian Kids.* Scholastic Canada, 2011.

Torpie, Kate. *Drawing Maps.* Crabtree Publishing Company, 2008.

Index